PICCOLO PICTURE BOOK OF FLAGS

PICCOLO PICTURE BOOK OF FLAGS

by

Valerie Pitt

Illustrated by Dorothy H. Ralphs

A Piccolo Picture Book

PAN BOOKS LTD : LONDON

There are all kinds of flags in the world . . .
all different colours and shapes. They fly high
over buildings, flutter from ships, flap in the
wind on top of mountains. There is even a flag
on the moon, planted there by the astronauts.

Flags are an easy way of giving information. Each flag has a different meaning. Each flag tells us something.

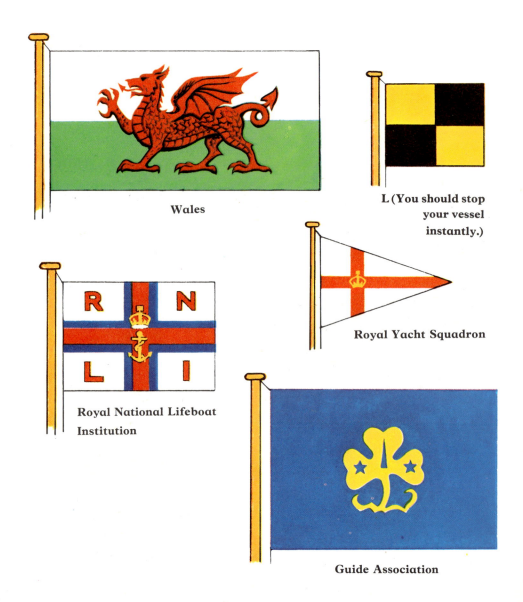

Wales

L (You should stop your vessel instantly.)

Royal Yacht Squadron

Royal National Lifeboat Institution

Guide Association

Some flags tell us about **people**.
Royalty and heads of countries often have their
  own flags. These are flown from their homes
  and on the cars and vessels they travel in.

This is Buckingham Palace, the Queen's home in London.

Outside, sentries and policemen stand guard. High above the Palace flies the Royal Standard, which stands for the Queen alone. This royal flag tells of the Queen's presence, for it is only flown from buildings where she is staying.

The Royal Standard is a very old flag and has been changed many times in its history. Today, it shows three symbols. The golden lions stand for England. The red lion stands for Scotland. And the golden harp stands for Ireland.

The Queen has a personal flag, too, showing the letter E, which is used on special occasions.

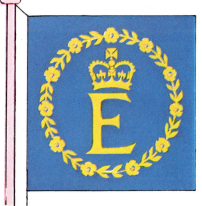

Some flags tell us about **countries**.

Here is a ship of the British Royal Navy at
anchor. From the bow, or front, of the
-ship flies the Union Jack. The flag is a sign
to everyone that the ship is British.

Every country is known by a different flag. These are called national flags and you can see some of them on pages 28–41. National flags are the most important flags of all. They symbolize the love people feel for their countries.

Some flags tell us about **organizations**.

This is a refugee camp. Nearby is a first-aid tent. The white flag with the red cross is the sign of the Red Cross, an organization which helps people in distress both in war-time and peace-time. On a battlefield this sign shows where medical help is available.

The Red Cross flag is used in many countries,
  but in Muslim countries a red crescent
  is used instead of a cross. One country, Iran,
  shows a red lion and sun as its symbol for the
  Red Cross organization.

Some flags tell us about **ideals**.

The United Nations works for world peace. Its
flag shows a map of the world, circled by olive
branches. Olive branches are an ancient sign
of peace.

This is the Olympic Games flag. The five circles
represent the five continents of the world. The
circles are linked together in a chain—a chain
is an ancient symbol of unity.

This is the Scout flag. The three branches of the lily symbolize the three promises boys make when they join the Scouts.

Some flags are used for **signalling**. Signalling
is a quick way of passing messages when
speaking or writing is impractical.

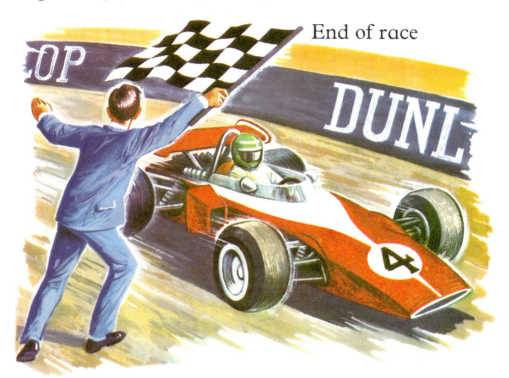

End of race

Racing drivers cannot stop during a race to
receive messages. They watch for different
flag signals as they zoom past the pits. Here
are some of them:

Oil on
the track

Driver
trying
to overtake

Stop

Ships have used flags to signal one another for hundreds of years. During the Battle of Trafalgar, Lord Nelson sent a famous message to spur on his fleet. The flags spelt out, "England expects that every man will do his duty."

Nelson's original message was "England confides that every man shall do his duty". The signaller pointed out he would have to spell out every letter of "confides", so Nelson changed it to "expects" for which there was an official code.

Today, all ships use the same International
Code of flag signals. There is a flag for each
letter of the alphabet and the numbers 0–9.

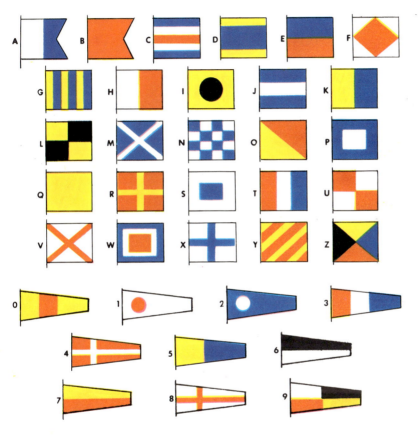

To save time, groups of flags are often flown
at once to spell out words. This is called a
hoist. Even if foreign ships pass messages
to each other they can still be understood.
Each ship carries a code book of the signals
printed in nine languages.

Some of the letter flags have separate meanings when they are flown on their own. The letter P, known as the Blue Peter, means the ship is about to put to sea. The letter O means man overboard. The letter D means difficulty in steering.

Messages are still sometimes passed to ships close-by with semaphore signals, too. Two flags are held in different positions to represent letters of the alphabet, so whole sentences can be spelt out.

Sometimes signals are passed by positioning
flags in different ways. If you see a flag at
half-mast, it is a sign of mourning.

A flag flown beneath a black ball at sea is a distress signal. It means that help is needed urgently.

Before the invention of radio, flags were important signals on the battlefield. In the crush of the fighting they helped leaders to spot the position of their men. And as they waved in the breeze they showed which way the wind was blowing—this helped the men to aim their spears and arrows.

Some colours are used as signals. A black flag
may be a sign of death or mourning. Black
flags were once shown in British prisons after
an execution. Pirates used to add a white
skull and cross-bones to a black flag.

A red flag is often a warning sign. Ships
carrying explosives often fly a red flag as a
danger signal. Red flags often mean
revolution, too. Russia adopted a red flag
after the Communist revolution in 1917.

A white flag can mean peace or surrender.

SOME NATIONAL FLAGS

AUSTRALIA

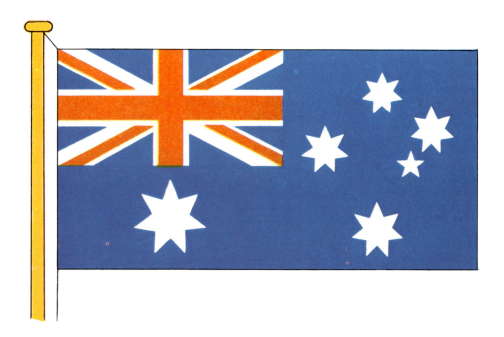

A member of the Commonwealth, Australia
shows its links with Britain by having the
Union Jack in the top corner of its flag. The
large star has points for each of the six
Australian states and one point for the rest of
the country which is ruled by the Australian
government. The five stars on the right of the
flag are patterned after the Southern Cross, a
group of stars sometimes seen in Australia.

AUSTRIA

In 1191, Duke Leopold V of Austria was wounded in battle. As he removed his blood-soaked tunic he found that one strip remained white, where his belt had been. Thus, he took a red flag with a white stripe across the centre as his emblem. This became the Austrian national flag in 1918.

BRITAIN

Union Jack

The flag of the United Kingdom, known as the Union Jack, is made up of three crosses. The red cross stands for St. George, the patron saint of England. The white diagonal cross stands for St. Andrew, patron saint of Scotland. The red diagonal cross stands for St. Patrick, patron saint of Ireland.

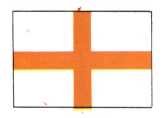

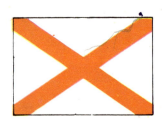

St. George   St. Andrew   St. Patrick

These are other British flags:

The White ensign,
flown by the Royal Navy.

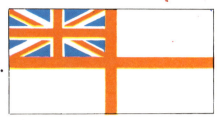

The Blue Ensign,
flown by the Royal Naval
Reserve.

The Royal Air Force
Ensign.

The Red Ensign,
flown by British
merchant ships.

. . . and the Army Flag.

BOLIVIA

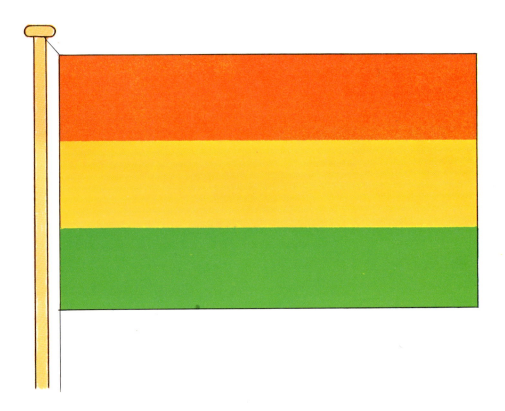

This country in South America has many
   natural resources. Its flag symbolizes this
   wealth. The red stripe stands for animals, the
   yellow stands for minerals and the green for
   agriculture.

CANADA

Canada was originally populated by people
from the British Isles and France and its flag
used to show these links. In 1965 a new flag
was designed because the people of Canada
thought their national flag should symbolize
Canada alone. A maple leaf was the original
symbol of Canada.

CHINA

The mainland of China is Communist. The small stars represent the four different types of workers in the country.

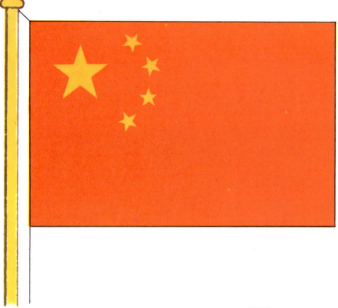

The island of Taiwan is called Nationalist China and has a different non-Communist flag which shows a white sun emblem.

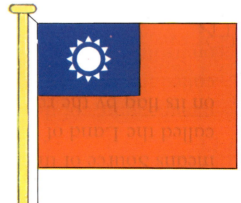

CYPRUS

This is the only country which shows a map on
its national flag. Under the shape of the island
of Cyprus, are two olive branches, ancient
signs of peace.

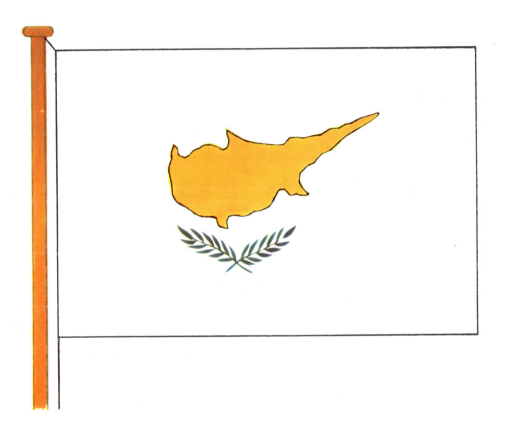

DENMARK

This is the oldest national flag. King Waldemar the Victorious, an ancient Danish ruler, was said to have seen a white cross in a red sky just before he won an important battle. This sign became the Danish national flag in 1219.

FRANCE

The blue, white and red flag of France is known
as the Tricolour. It has been the symbol of
France since the French Revolution in the
18th century. Many revolutionary flags have
three bands of colour like this.

ISRAEL

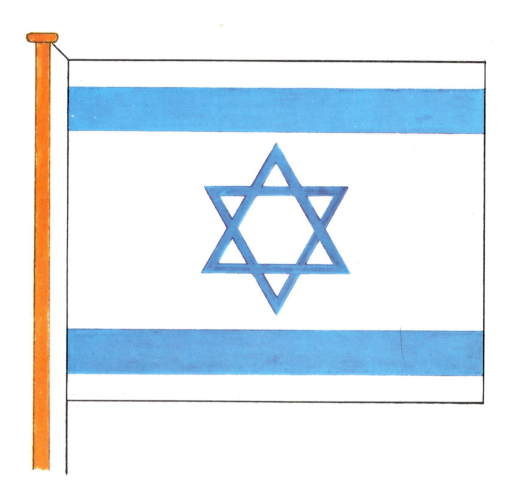

The Jewish state of Israel has a flag which shows a six-pointed star called the Star of David. It is an ancient Jewish symbol of King David who ruled the Jews 3,000 years ago.

JAPAN

In Japanese this country is called Nippon, which
means Source of the Sun. Japan is often
called the Land of the Rising Sun, symbolized
on its flag by the red ball.

This red revolutionary flag was adopted in 1917
when the Communists took over Russia. The
gold star represents unity among the five
continents and the hammer and sickle stand
for the factory and farm workers.

UNITED STATES

The famous Stars and Stripes has 50 stars to
represent the 50 states that make up the
United States. The 13 stripes stand for the
original 13 states.

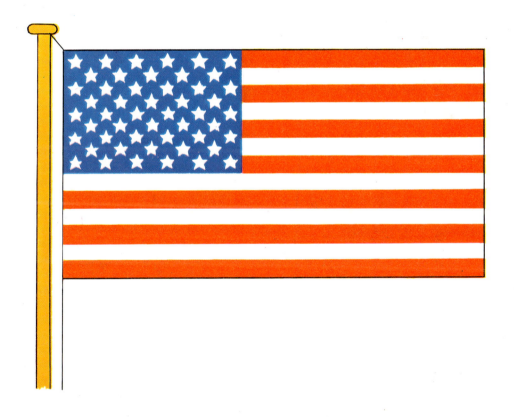

SOME FLAG TERMS

BURGEE
A flag shaped at the ends.

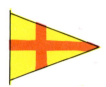

CLUB BURGEE
Club burgee is a pennant

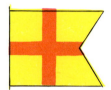

COMMODORE'S BURGEE
Commodore's burgee is a swallow tail

COURTESY FLAG
When a ship enters a foreign port, she hoists
that country's national flag to her cross trees
as a sign of respect and lowers it on leaving.

DIPPING A FLAG
Lowering a flag and then raising it again.
Ships salute each other in this way at sea.

ENSIGN

The flag flown at the stern (or rear) of a ship and even of small boats. In some countries the ensign is the national flag, in others a specially designed flag. The British Royal Navy flies the White Ensign, and the Merchant Navy the Red Ensign.

FLEUR DE LYS

A French term meaning the lily flower. It used to be a symbol of French royalty.

FLY

The part of the flag farthest from the flagstaff.

HOIST

The part of the flag nearest to the flagstaff.

JACK

A flag flown at the bow (or front) of a ship.

MERCHANT FLAG

A flag flown by all vessels not in government
 service.

PENNANT

A flag that ends in a point.

STRIKING A FLAG

Lowering the flag as a sign of surrender in
 war-time.

Flags have been used for thousands of years. They have spurred people on in war-time. They have inspired courage and sacrifice. Many men and women have died for their flags. That is why flags are always treated with respect.

INDEX